Read and Do Science

HOT and COLD

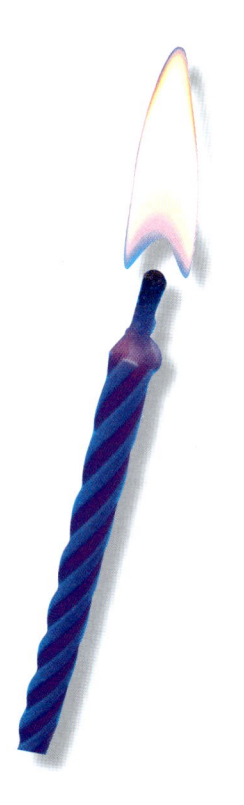

Written by Melinda Lilly
Photos by Scott M. Thompson
Design by Elizabeth Bender

Educational Consultants

Kimberly Weiner, Ed.D

Betty Carter, Ed.D

Maria Czech, Ph.D
California State University Northridge

Rourke
Publishing LLC

Vero Beach, Florida 32964

Before You Read This Book

Think about these facts:

1. Think of a time when you were too cold. What did you do to warm up?
2. What does it feel like when you touch something hot? Compare a cold drink with a hot one.

The experiments in this book should be undertaken with adult supervision.

For the Weismans

—M. L. and S. T.

©2006 Rourke Publishing LLC

All rights reserved. No part of this book may be reproduced or utilized in any form or by any means, electronic, or mechanical including photocopying, recording, or by any information storage and retrieval system without permission in writing from the publisher.

Library of Congress Cataloging-in-Publication Data

Lilly, Melinda
 Hot and Cold / Lilly, Melinda.
   p. cm. -- (Read and do science)
 ISBN 1-59515-402-7 (hardcover)

Printed in the USA

Table of Contents

Once Upon a Time 4
You Are Your Own Thermometer! 6
What's Hot? 7
Judging Temperature 12
How Dew You Dew? 15
It's Dew Cold! 17
Where Did the Water Come From? 21
Glossary 22
Take It Further: Melting 23
Think About It! 24
Index 24

Once upon a time . . .

Goldilocks had a problem with **temperature.**

Too cold!

How can Goldilocks—or you—judge temperature?

You don't carry a **thermometer** around with you, do you?

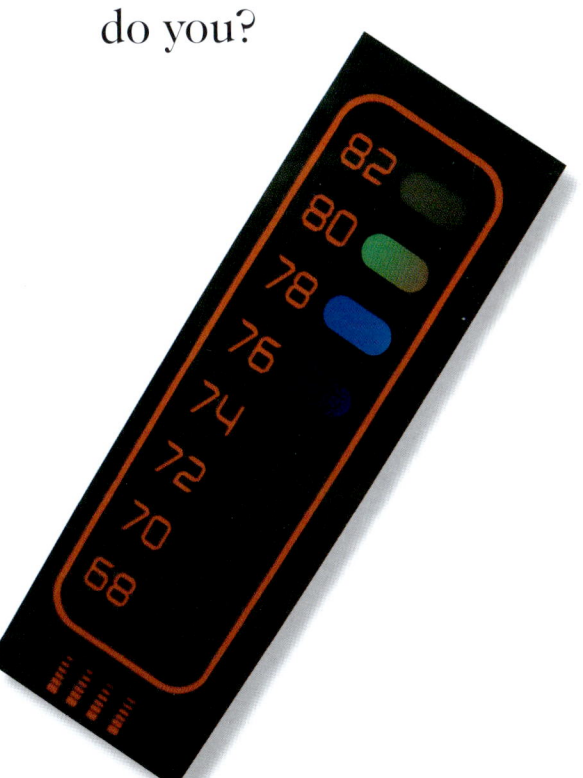

You Are Your Own Thermometer!

Unless you have a fever, the temperature inside your body stays at 98.6 degrees **Fahrenheit** (37 degrees **Celsius**). You compare your temperature with whatever you touch.

Find out how well you judge hot and cold!

What's Hot?

What You Need:
- Different materials, such as wood, glass, Styrofoam, metal, and flannel; do not use anything that has been heated or chilled
- An aquarium thermometer strip
- A clock

Gather the items. Place them out of the sunshine. Wait five minutes.

Touch each object.

Too hot!

Too cold!

Just right, thanks!

Line up the items from warmest to coolest. Pile up everything that seems to be the same temperature.

Place the thermometer on each item. The highest number next to a bright color is the temperature.

Is everything the same temperature? That's the temperature where you are.

Judging Temperature

Why did some things feel cooler than others when all are the same temperature?

How hot or cold something feels depends how well it **conducts** or moves heat through itself.

Metal conducts heat quickly. Touch it. The warmth from your hand spreads rapidly through the metal. The spot where your hand touches the metal feels cool.

Flannel is an **insulator.** It does not conduct heat. The warmth from your hand stays on the spot where you touch the flannel. It and your hand feel like the same temperature.

That's one reason pajamas are made of flannel instead of metal!

Cozy!

How Dew You Dew?

Dew glistens on cool mornings. What makes dew?

Water vapor is water in the air. It's a gas. When the temperature dips and there is enough water vapor, it changes into a liquid—dew.

The temperature at which water vapor turns into dew is called the **dew point.** When the air is dry, it must get colder to make dew.

Figure out the dew point of your room!

It's Dew Cold!

What You Need:
- A can half full of water that's warmer than the room and cooler than 98.6 degrees Fahrenheit (37 degrees Celsius)
- An aquarium thermometer that can measure up to 100 degrees Fahrenheit (38 degrees Celsius) and down to the freezing point of 32 degrees (0 degrees Celsius)
- A thermometer strip for an aquarium
- Three ice cubes
- Paper
- Pencil

Read the strip to learn the temperature of the room. (For directions, see page 11.)

Put the other thermometer in the water.

Read the number next to the highest point of the red line. That's the water temperature.

Write it down.

Drop the ice cubes in the water.

When dew appears on the outside of the can, check the temperature. You've figured out the dew point of the room!

Where Did the Water Come From?

The can cooled to the dew point. Water vapor **condensed** into dew on the can.

Dew

You made water appear out of thin air! Not too shabby for someone who's part thermometer!

Glossary

Celsius (SELL see us) — a scale for measuring temperature that puts the freezing point at zero degrees

condensed (kon DENS) — to have changed from a gas into a liquid

conducts (kon DUKTS) — to transfer heat from one place to another

dew point (DYOO POYNT) — the temperature at which water vapor becomes liquid

Fahrenheit (FAR en hiyt) — a scale for measuring temperature that puts the freezing point at 32 degrees

insulator (IN soo layt ur) — something that does not conduct heat

melting point (MELT ing POYNT) — the temperature at which something melts

temperature (TEM per uh cher) — a measurement of hot and cold

thermometer (ther MOM ih ter) — an instrument that measures temperature

water vapor (WA ter VAY por) — water when it is a gas

Take It Further: Melting

1. Collect a chocolate chip, plus a broken crayon and a chunk of ice, both about the same size as the chocolate chip.

2. Put each one in a clear plastic baggie.

3. Set them in the sun.

4. Write down the temperature (as shown on the thermometer strip) and the time.

5. How long does it take the ice to melt? How about the chocolate and the crayon? Write down the times and the temperatures.

6. Which one started melting first? That is the item with the lowest **melting point.**

Think About It!

1. How are the melting point and the dew point similar? How are they different?

2. Which do you think would best conduct heat, socks or scissors? Why?

3. Which would have a lower dew point, the desert or a rain forest? Why?

Index

dew point 16, 17, 20, 21, 22, 24

insulator 14, 22

temperature 4, 5, 6, 10, 11, 12, 14, 15, 16, 18, 19, 20, 22, 23

thermometer 5, 6, 7, 11, 17, 18, 21, 22, 23

water vapor 15, 16, 21, 22

LONG BRANCH ES APS,VA

66437985   536 L11
Hot and cold